MEXICAN
authentic cooking

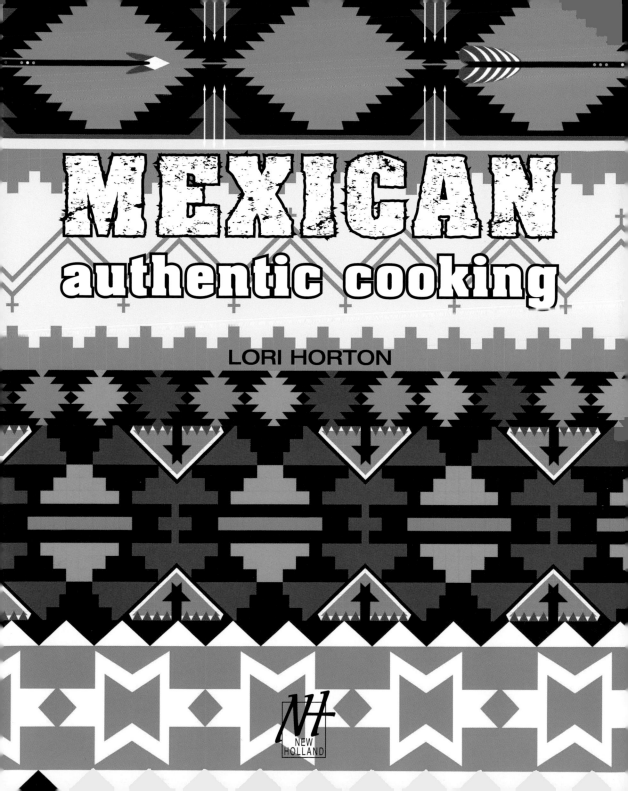

MEXICAN
authentic cooking

LORI HORTON

NEW HOLLAND

Contents

To my daughter Maliah,

You have enriched and brought so much joy to our lives.

Introduction

Mexican culture and food is vast, varied, stimulating, festive and rich and to truly appreciate Mexican cooking, it's necessary to understand Mexico's history and geography. Many of the foods in the Mexican pantry carry ancient history. Traditional staples of the Aztecs and Mayans were items such as beans, tomatoes, corn, and chilli peppers and they rank among the world's first cultivated foods. Later, the Spanish conquerors introduced wheat, herbs, spices and dairy foods to the pantry. Over the centuries, Mexican cuisine has emerged out of this as a fusion of ingredients and techniques.

Here are some of the ingredients you should keep in your cupboard to create quick and easy Mexican meals. Many of these ingredients can be found in farmers markets, supermarkets and speciality stores.

Dried beans – A Mexican staple dating back to pre-Columbian times, beans are a common accompaniment on Mexican dinner plates. They're often prepared simply by simmering them in water, perhaps with fresh herbs like epazote, a native wild herb. The term 'refried beans' actually refers to them being well-fried, not fried again.

Tortillas – For centuries, corn was ground, turned into dough (*masa*) and then shaped into small, very thin cakes called tortillas. After the Spanish introduced wheat into Mexico, flour tortillas became known. Whether corn- or flour-based, tortillas are stuffed with meats, stews, beans and rice, and eaten like tacos; or filled, rolled and baked as enchiladas or deep-fried as chimichangas.

Chilli peppers – There are many varieties of chilli peppers, from mild Anaheims to fiery hot habañeros, and they all have their uses in Mexican cuisine. Generally the smaller the chilli, the hotter it is. Green jalapeños—from Jalapa, the capital of Veracruz—are the most known. When they mature, they turn red or purple in colour. Once dried and smoked, jalapeños become chipotle chillies. Large poblano chillies are green. When left to mature on the vine to a red colour and then dried, they become an ancho chilli. A pasilla chilli is a fresh chilaca pepper that has been dried and turns black in colour.

Tomatillo – Sometimes called Mexican green tomatoes or husk tomatoes, although they are not botanically related, fresh tomatillos are covered in thin husks. Their taste is tart, and they are often roasted or boiled and used in salsa.

Nopales – Prickly pear (nopal) cactus leaves are eaten fresh, canned, pickled and candied. Once these have been peeled they are safe to handle.

Annatto (Achiote) – These are the bright red seeds that come from a tropical bush that grows in Mexico. Ground into seasoning pastes, annatto seeds add deep red colour and pungent flavour to Mexican dishes.

Chilli powder – In other cuisines, the term chilli powder refers to a single ground red chilli, such as cayenne. Mexican chilli powder is a particular spice blend made from different dried chillies, Mexican oregano, cumin, coriander/cilantro, and sometimes garlic, cloves and salt.

Cumin – Cumin has a strong musty, earthy flavour with some grassy notes. Cumin is an important ingredient of chilli powder, achiote and adobo sauce.

Epazote or wormseed – is a herb that is native to Central America, South America as well as Southern Mexico. It has a pleasant flavour and is commonly used with black beans.

Mexican oregano – Milder than Mediterranean versions, Mexican oregano is found in chilli powders, chilli con carne and other Mexican dishes.

Tabasco sauce – This famous sauce is made from Tabasco chillies. Created by Edmund McIlhenny in Louisiana in 1868, much the same Tabasco sauce is still produced there today.

My family and I have travelled the world eating Mexican food, searching out new recipes and flavours to create. I hope you enjoy the authentic Mexican food of *Mexicali Rose*.

Lori Horton

DIPS

Guacamole

MAKES APPROX 2 CUPS

2 tablespoons onion, diced
¼ hot fresh green Serrano chillies
1 tablespoon fresh coriander/cilantro
½ teaspoon salt
½ tablespoon letmon juice
4 avocados, peeled, seeded and mashed
2 medium-sized roma tomatoes, diced

In a food processor, blend the onion, chilli, coriander/cilantro, salt and lemon juice until smooth. Add the avocado and tomato to the blended ingredients and mix thoroughly.

Place in a serving bowl and serve with warm corn chips.

Note:
The avocado has been cultivated in Mexico for at least 5,000 years. Unripened avocados will not ripen in the refrigerator; they're best left in a paper bag at room temperature until soft.

CHIPOTLE DIP

MAKES ABOUT 1½ CUPS

2 spring onions/scallions, finely chopped
1½ teaspoons chipotle peppers in adobo sauce (available in tins from specialty suppliers)
1 cup (250ml) mayonnaise
½ cup (175ml) sour cream
1 teaspoon fresh lemon juice
salt to taste

- -

In a medium-sized bowl, whisk together all the ingredients.

Place in a serving bowl and serve with corn chips or a tray of crisp, fresh vegetables.

NOTE:
Dip may be kept, covered and chilled for up to 3 days.

Mexican Layered Dip

SERVES 8

1 x 400g (13oz) can red kidney beans, drained and rinsed
pepper to taste
2 small tomatoes, chopped
2 spring onions/scallions, chopped
2 small avocados, chopped
¼ cup fresh coriander/cilantro leaves, chopped
1 small red chilli, deseeded, finely chopped
1 tablespoon lime juice
½ cup (60g) grated cheese
½ cup (125ml) extra light sour cream
chopped fresh coriander/cilantro leaves to garnish

- -

Place the beans in a bowl. Using the back of a fork, lightly mash them and season with pepper. Stir in the tomato and spring onions/scallions.

Place avocado in a bowl. Add the coriander/cilantro, chilli and lime juice. Mash until smooth.

Place the bean mixture in the base of a medium-sized glass bowl. Put a layer of avocado mixture on top. Top with the cheese and sour cream and garnish with coriander/cilantro.

Place in a serving bowl and serve with warm corn chips.

Note:
Introduced by the Spanish, the herb cilantro is the green leaves of the coriander plant. Fresh cilantro is featured in many Mexican dishes and is a must in salsas. Cooked, it loses its taste and appearance, therefore ideally it is added to dishes just before serving.

CHILE CON QUESO

MAKES 2 CUPS

110g (3¾oz) butter
210g (7½oz) onions, finely diced
140g (5oz) green capsicum/green sweet pepper, diced
½ x 375ml (12 fl oz) can evaporated milk
500g (1lb) processed cheddar cheese, finely grated
1 tablespoon pickled jalapeños (optional) (available from supermarkets and specialty stores)

- -

In a small saucepan, melt the butter and sauté the onion and capsicum/sweet pepper until the onion is semi-translucent.

Add the evaporated milk and heat until hot, stirring regularly, but do not let it boil. Add the cheese and fold through until the cheese is melted. Remove the saucepan from the heat and stir through the jalapeños.

Pour into a serving bowl and serve with warm corn chips.

Jalapeño Black Bean Dip

MAKES APPROX 2 CUPS

1 cup black beans
½ teaspoon epazote (available from specialty suppliers)
1 teaspoon crushed garlic
¼ teaspoon diced pickled jalapeños
¼ teaspoon ground cumin
pinch of salt
2 tablespoons white vinegar

- -

In a bowl add the beans and 3 cups (750ml) of water. Set aside to soak for 2 hours, then drain. Place the beans in a saucepan with 4 cups (1 litre) of cold water and bring to the boil. Reduce the heat and simmer for 1 hour. Drain the beans and run under col water to cool.

Place all ingredients in food processor and blend until smooth.

Place in a serving bowl and serve with warm corn chips. This dip can be served warm or cold.

NOTE:
You can get epazote at specialist grocers.
It is a herb with a pungent flavour, rather
like fresh coriander/cilantro.

SOUPS

CREAM OF JALAPEÑO SOUP

SERVES 4

7 jalapeño peppers, stemmed, seeded and finely diced
1 cup sweet yellow onion, finely diced
2 tablespoons butter
1 tablespoon garlic, minced
½ cup avocado, diced
2 cups fresh or roasted tomatoes, diced
8 cups (2 litres) thickened cream
cracked black pepper to taste
1 bunch coriander/cilantro, stemmed and chopped
chilli for garnish

- -

Cook the jalapeño and onion in butter in a heavy-based frying pan. Add the garlic and stir until
the onion is translucent. Add the avocado, tomato and cream. Cook at a gentle simmer for
30 minutes, stirring often to keep the liquid from burning. Remove the pan from the heat and
allow to cool.

Add the mixture to a blender and blend until smooth. Add a generous amount of pepper and
blend in the coriander/cilantro. Place in serving bowls and garnish with coriander leaves and chilli.

GAZPACHO

SERVES 4

50g (2oz) day-old white bread, crusts removed, broken into pieces
½ cup (125ml) water
4 cups ripe tomatoes, roughly chopped
1 small cucumber, peeled, roughly chopped
½ red capsicum/red sweet pepper, deseeded, roughly chopped
2 garlic cloves
½ cup (125ml) extra virgin olive oil (preferably Spanish)
¼ cup (60ml) sherry vinegar
½ teaspoon salt, or to taste
½ teaspoon sugar, or to taste
1 ripe tomato, extra, deseeded, diced, to serve
1 cucumber, extra, deseeded, diced, to serve
extra virgin olive oil (preferably Spanish), extra, to serve

- -

In a small bowl place the bread and pour the the water over it. Set aside for 5 minutes to soak. In a colander, drain the bread and place it between paper towel to absorb any excess moisture.

Place the bread in a food processor. Add the tomato, cucumber, capsicum/sweet pepper and garlic and process until well combined and almost smooth. Add the oil and vinegar and continue to process until all the ingredients are well combined. Add salt and sugar to season.

Pass the soup through a sieve into a bowl, using a wooden spoon to press down firmly to extract all the liquid. Discard the pulp. Cover the soup and place in the fridge for 2 hours or until well chilled.

Ladle the soup into small bowls, top with the extra diced tomato and cucumber, and drizzle with a little of the extra oil. Serve immediately.

Sopa de Tortilla (Tortilla Soup)

SERVES 4

1 cup dried kidney beans
6 large ripe tomatoes
1 small red chilli, deseeded, coarsely chopped
1 red onion, coarsely chopped
1 litre (4 cups) chicken stock
2 corn cobs, husk and silks removed
2 tablespoons lime juice
2 tablespoons olive oil

- -

Place beans in a large bowl and cover with plenty of cold water. Set aside overnight to soak. Drain beans and place in a saucepan. Cover the beans with fresh water and bring to the boil. Cook for 30 minutes or until the beans are tender. Drain well.

Blanch tomatoes by carefully dropping them in boiling water for 10 seconds. Using a slotted spoon, transfer the tomatoes to a bowl of cold water to refresh. Remove the skins and coarsely chop. In a food processor, place the tomato, chilli and onion and process until almost smooth.

Transfer the tomato mixture to a large saucepan. Cook on medium heat for 10 minutes, stirring occasionally, or until the mixture thickens slightly. Add stock and bring to a simmer. Cook for a further 10 minutes or until soup thickens slightly.

Use a small, sharp knife to cut kernels from the corn cobs. Add the corn kernels, beans and lime juice to the saucepan and stir to combine. Bring back to a simmer. Taste and season with salt, pepper and extra lime juice if desired.

Heat oil in a frying pan on high heat. Add one-third of the tortilla strips and cook until golden and crisp. Transfer to a plate lined with paper towel. Repeat in two more batches with the remaining strips.

In a small bowl combine the fetta, avocado and coriander/cilantro. Ladle the soup into serving bowls. Top with the avocado mixture and serve with the tortillas and lime wedges. This soup can be served hot or cold.

SALADS

Mexican Chicken Salad

SERVES 2 AS A MAIN COURSE OR 4 AS A SIDE SALAD

2 cups cooked chicken, cut into cubes
½ red capsicum/red sweet pepper, chopped
½ head lettuce chopped
½ apple, cored and chopped
¼ cup red onion, chopped
8 green olives, halved
fresh basil for garnish

Dressing

6 tablespoons mayonnaise
2 teaspoons lime juice
1 teaspoon honey
salt and pepper to taste

- -

To make the salad, in a medium-sized bowl combine the chicken, capsicum/sweet pepper, lettuce, apple, onion and olives.

To make the dressing, in another bowl mix the mayonnaise, lime juice and honey. Add more honey or lime juice to taste. Add salt and pepper to taste.

Combine the salad with the dressing and serve in bowls garnished with basil.

Ensalada de Naranjas (Mandarin Salad)

SERVES 2

¾ teaspoon salt
¾ teaspoon chilli powder
¾ tablespoon sugar
¼ cup (60ml) white vinegar
¼ onion, sliced
1 × 425g (15oz) can of mandarin segments
½ cos/romaine lettuce, roughly chopped
1 red tomato, cut into wedges, to serve
½ small cucumber, sliced, to serve
1 small red chilli, deseeded and sliced

Dressing
¼ teaspoon salt
¼ teaspoon chilli powder
1 teaspoon sugar
¼ cup (60ml) white vinegar
¼ cup (60ml) oil

To make the dressing, mix all the ingredients in a small jar by shaking well. Place in the refrigerator to chill.

To make the salad, in a large bowl place all the ingredients, except for the lettuce, and mix well. Refrigerate the salad to chill.

Just before serving, gently toss the lettuce into the salad. Add the dressing to salad and garnish with cucumber slices and tomato wedges.

Ensalada de Nopalitos (Cactus Salad)

SERVES 6

500g (1lb) nopales (pickled cactus), drained and rinsed (available at specialist grocers)
1 small onion
2 tomatoes, peeled and diced,
¼ cup coriander/cilantro, chopped
¼ cup (60ml) olive oil
juice of 1 lemon
3 tablespoons white vinegar
2 teaspoons oregano
salt to taste
pepper to taste
½ cup crumbled fetta cheese
½ iceberg lettuce, roughly chopped
chillies, chopped for garnish (optional)
coriander/cilantro for garnish

- -

In a large bowl, combine well all the ingredients, except the lettuce.

Place the lettuce in a serving bowl or arrange on a platter. Place the nopale mixture on top.

Garnish with coriander/cilantro and serve. Add the chilli if you like it hot.

STARTERS

Nachos

SERVES 4 TO 6

10 cups (300g) corn chips
3 cups (375g) grated cheddar cheese
2 tablespoons pickled jalapeños, chopped (optional)
2 cups (500g) tomato salsa (see page 84)
¾ cup (180ml) guacamole (see page 12)
¾ cup (180ml) sour cream
½ small red capsicum/red sweet pepper, finely diced, for garnish
spring onion/scallions, sliced, for garnish

- -

Preheat oven to 180°C (350°F).

Place the corn chips on a large plate or casserole dish or on individual plates. Layer evenly with the cheese and sprinkle with the jalapeño. Bake in the oven for 10 to 15 minutes until all the cheese has melted evenly and is just starting to turn golden. Remove from the oven and top with the salsa, guacamole and sour cream. Garnish with capsicum/sweet pepper and spring onions/scallions and serve immediately.

POTATO TORTILLA

SERVES 8

¼ cup (60ml) olive oil
200g (7oz) proscuitto, cut into 1cm pieces
1 brown onion, halved, thinly sliced
4 garlic cloves, crushed
3 (about 600g or 1lb) desiree potatoes, peeled, thinly sliced
8 eggs
salt to taste
freshly ground black pepper to taste

- -

Heat 1 tablespoon of oil in a 30-cm (12-in) frying pan over medium-high heat. Add the proscuitto, onion and garlic and cook, stirring, for 10 minutes or until onion softens. Transfer to a bowl and set aside.

Heat the remaining oil in the same frying pan. Add the potato and cook, stirring occasionally, for 25 minutes or until the potatoes are golden brown and tender.

Meanwhile, whisk the eggs in a medium-sized bowl until combined. Season with salt and pepper to taste. Preheat the grill on high.

Sprinkle the onion mixture over the potato mixture in the pan. Pour the egg over the top. Cook over medium-high heat for 8 minutes or until the base of the tortilla is golden and set. As it cooks, shake the pan gently to loosen the tortilla from the base of the pan.

Place the tortilla in the pan under the grill, about 6cm (2½in) from the heat source, and cook for 5 minutes or until golden and set. Use a round-blade knife to loosen the edges of the tortilla. Set aside for 5 minutes to cool. Cut into wedges and serve.

NOTE:
The onion mixture can be prepared up to 6 hours ahead.
The rest of the recipe can be prepared up to 3 hours ahead.

Jalapeño Cornbread

SERVES 8

2 eggs, lightly whisked
1 cup (250ml) buttermilk
1 tablespoon olive oil plus extra olive oil to grease
1 cup plain/all purpose flour
1 tablespoon baking powder/baking soda
1 cup instant polenta/cornmeal
1 teaspoon salt
2 x 125g (4oz) cans corn kernels, rinsed, drained
2 fresh jalapeños, halved, deseeded, finely chopped
1½ cups coarsely grated cheddar

- -

Preheat oven to 160°C (325°F). Grease a 6-cm deep, 20 x 9cm loaf pan. Line the base and sides with non-stick baking paper.

Combine the eggs, buttermilk and extra oil in a large jug and set aside.

Sift the flour and baking powder/baking soda into a large bowl. Stir in the polenta and salt. Make a well in the centre of the mixture. Gradually add the egg mixture, stirring until smooth. Stir in the corn kernels, jalapeño and three-quarters of the cheese. Pour the mixture into the loaf pan and sprinkle with the remaining cheese.

Bake for 25–35 minutes or until a metal skewer inserted into the centre comes out clean. Set aside in the pan for 5 minutes to cool before turning onto a wire rack.

Cut into slices and serve.

Note:
This dish can be made up to 5 hours ahead and stored at room temperature.

QUESADILLA DE TINGA

MAKES 20 PIECES

1 tablespoon oil
½ onion, diced
2 cloves garlic, crushed
1 x 400g (13oz) can diced tomato, drained
2 chipotle peppers in adobo sauce, finely chopped (available in tins from specialty suppliers)
¼ teaspoon salt
20 x 12cm (4½in) corn tortillas
2½ cups (300g) grated cheddar cheese

- -

Preheat oven to 180°C (350°F).

Heat the oil in a small pot. Add the onion and garlic and cook until translucent. Then add the tomatoes, chillies and salt and cook for 10 minutes.

Meanwhile, heat some oil in a frying pan. Lightly fry the tortillas until they begin to brown but are still soft.

Fill the tortillas with an even amount of the tomato mix, top with the grated cheese and fold them in half. Place on a baking tray and bake in the oven for 10 to 15 minutes until slightly crisp. Serve on a bed of lettuce with guacamole.

Hot & Spicy Chicken Drumettes

MAKES APPROX 12 PIECES

1kg (2lb) chicken drumettes

Sauce
1 cup (250ml) salad oil
¾ cup (180ml) Tabasco sauce
1 cup (250ml) tomato sauce
¼ cup (60ml) bottled lemon juice
1 tablespoon Dijon mustard
1 cup brown sugar
¹/₃ tablespoon salt
sour cream, to serve

To make the sauce, combine all the ingredients well using a whisk. Set aside a quarter of the sauce for dipping.

Place the chicken drumettes in a large bowl. Pour over the remaining sauce, making sure the chicken is well covered, and refrigerate overnight for best results.

Preheat oven to 200°C (400°F). Place drumettes on a wire rack with a tray underneath. Cook for 15 minutes. Turn and cook for a further 15 minutes.

Serve with dipping sauce and sour cream on the side.

Note:
This is best made the day before. Marinate the chicken overnight for the best flavour.

VEGETARIAN

ENCHILADAS DE ESPINACA

MAKES APPROX 6 PIECES

1 cup frozen chopped spinach
1 teaspoon garlic
1 cup (250ml) sour cream
oil for frying
6 x 15cm (6in) corn tortillas
6 cups (1½ litres) chipotle chilli sauce (see page 81)
1 cup (125g) grated cheddar cheese
chopped onion for garnish
coriander/cilantro for garnish

- -

Preheat oven to 180°C (350°F).

Defrost the spinach in a colander to drain. Squeeze out excess liquid between paper towels. Combine the spinach, garlic and sour cream and mix well.

Heat some oil in a large frying pan. Lightly fry the tortillas until they begin to brown but are still soft.

Distribute the spinach mixture evenly among the tortillas and fold in half. Place the enchilades in a medium to large ovenproof casserole dish and pour the chipotle sauce over. Cover the dish with foil and bake for 30 minutes. Remove the foil and sprinkle with the grated cheese. Bake for a few more minutes until the cheese is melted.

Garnish with the onion and coriander/cilantro.

QUESADILLA GRANDE

SERVES 4

FILLING
4 x 25cm (10in) flour tortillas
1 onion, diced
½ cup pickled nopales, drained and diced (if desired) (available at specialist grocers)
4 tablespoons diced jalapeños (optional)
3 cups (750ml) tomato salsa (see page 84)
1 cup (250ml)w sour cream
4 cups (500g) grated cheddar cheese
2 tablespoons oil

- -

Place the tortillas on the bench. Evenly distribute the onion, nopales and jalapeños (if desired) among the tortillas. Top with the salsa, sour cream and cheese. Fold each tortilla in half.

In a frypan, heat the oil over a medium to low heat. Add the tortillas and pan fry until the ingredients inside are hot and it is a light, crisp, golden brown colour on the outside. Approximately 5 minutes each side. Serve immediately..

Tex Mex Style Beef Tacos

MAKES 12 TACOS

2 cups (500g) diced blade meat
¾ cup (180g) diced onions
¾ tablespoon garlic
¾ cup (180ml) water
1 teaspoon salt
12 taco shells
1 onion, diced
½ lettuce, shredded
3 cups tomato salsa (see page 84)
2 cups (250g) grated cheddar cheese

- -

In a heavy-based saucepan add the beef, onion, garlic and water and cover with a lid. Bring to boil then simmer for approximately 2 hours or until the meat is tender. Drain off two-thirds of the liquid. Add the salt. Using a fork, stir until the meat is shredded.

Heat the taco shells. These can be deep fried for 10 seconds each or placed in the oven, preheated to 180°C (350°F), for 2 to 3 minutes.

Layer the ingredients in the taco shell by adding approximately 2 tablespoons of the shredded beef, then the onion, lettuce and salsa. Add a sprinkle of grated cheese on top and serve immediately.

> **NOTE:**
> Other delicious toppings include diced tomato, guacamole and chopped jalapeños.
> Hard shell tacos do not actually exist in Mexico. The traditional way to prepare your tacos is in soft, warm corn tortillas.

Mexican Meatballs

SERVES 6

1kg (2lb) lean beef mince/grand beef
1 red onion, finely chopped
⅓ cup finely chopped fresh coriander/cilantro
1 egg
2 tablespoons taco seasoning
2 tablespoons olive oil
1 red capsicum/red sweet pepper, halved, deseeded and finely chopped
2 garlic cloves, crushed
2 × 400g (13oz) cans diced tomatoes
guacamole, to serve (see page 12)
sour cream, to serve
fresh coriander sprigs, to serve
flour tortillas, to serve

- -

Combine the mince, onion, coriander/cilantro, egg and half the taco seasoning in a bowl. Roll a tablespoon of mince mixture into a ball and transfer to a plate. Repeat with the remaining mince.

Heat 1 tablespoon of the oil in a large non-stick frying pan over medium-high heat. Add one-third of the meatballs and cook, turning, for 4–5 minutes or until golden. Transfer to a clean plate. Repeat, in 2 more batches with the remaining meatballs, reheating the pan between batches.

Heat the remaining tablespoon of oil in the pan over medium heat. Add the capsicum/sweet pepper, and garlic and cook, stirring, for 3 minutes or until the capsicum is soft. Add the remaining taco seasoning and cook, stirring, for 1 minute. Stir in the tomato. Reduce the heat and simmer, stirring occasionally, for 5 minutes. Add the meatballs and simmer for a further 5 minutes or until the sauce thickens slightly.

Divide the meatballs among serving bowls. Top with guacamole, sour cream and coriander. Serve with flour tortillas.

CHILLI CON CARNE

MAKES 4 CUPS

1 tablespoon olive oil
500g (1lb) minced beef/ground beef
1 small onion, diced
1 x 400g (13oz) can tomato puree/tomato paste
½ teaspoon salt
1 teaspoon chilli powder
¼ teaspoon cumin
½ cup (125ml) water
¼ teaspoon white sugar
25ml (1 fl oz) white vinegar
¼ teaspoon meat seasoning
1 x 400g (13oz) can crushed tomato
1 x 400g (13oz) can kidney beans, drained

Heat the oil in a large pot on. Add the mince beef and onions and brown.

In a small bowl mix the tomato puree, salt, chilli powder, cumin, sugar, white vinegar and meat seasoning in a bowl and add the water. Whisk until smooth. Add the spice mix to the mince. Then add the crushed tomato and kidney beans and stir well. Simmer until the meat is thoroughly cooked, approximately 45 minutes. Place in a serving bowl and serve with corn chips. Also great as a dip, topped with grated cheese and sour cream or burrito filling.

TIP:
A bowl of chilli con carne makes a great light lunch served with flour tortillas.

CHICKEN

Tortilla with Guacamole & Chipotle Spiced Chicken

MAKES 4 TORTILLAS

1 tablespoon oil
2 chicken breasts, halved
2 chipotle peppers in adobo sauce, finely diced (available in tins from specialty suppliers)
2 teaspoons chilli powder
salt and pepper
1 mango, peeled and stoned
1 avocado, peeled and stoned
1 clove garlic, crushed
juice of one lime
2 tablespoons chopped coriander/cilantro, plus extra to garnish
1 jalapeño
4 x 15cm (6in) flour tortillas
1 iceberg lettuce, sliced
tomatoes, chopped

- -

Heat the oil in a frying pan. Mix the chipotle peppers, chilli powder, salt and pepper together and rub onto the chicken breast halves. Sauté the chicken until golden brown and cooked right through. Remove the pan from the heat and leave to cool for 5 minutes. Cut the chicken into cubes.

To make the guacamole, place three-quarters of the mango, all of the avocado, garlic, lime juice, coriander and jalapeño in a food processor and puree. Cut the remaining mango into slices. Set aside.

Warm the tortilla in the microwave or in a dry frying pan over medium heat. Place the tortillas on a plate and evenly divide the chicken on top. Top with lettuce, tomato and a tablespoon of guacamole. Garnish with the mango slices and coriander/cilantro. Serve with salsa and sour cream on the side.

Pollo Con Avocado

SERVES 4

100ml (3½ fl oz) achiote paste (available from speciality grocers)
¾ cup (180ml) orange juice
4 large chicken breast fillets, skin removed
3 tablespoons oil
Mexican rice, to serve (see page 79)
salsa verde, to serve (see page 85)
guacamole, to serve (see page 12)
pico de gallo, to serve (see page 84)
½ red capsicum/red sweet pepper, diced, for garnish
coriander/cilantro, for garnish

- -

In a large bowl, mix the achiote paste and orange juice together until smooth. Add the chicken fillets, making sure chicken is completely covered, and marinate for 1–2 hours.

Preheat oven 180°C (350°F). Heat the oil in a large frying pan. Add the chicken and seal on both sides by turning quickly. Place the chicken in lightly greased casserole dish, cover with foil and bake in the oven for approximately 30 minutes or until chicken is cooked.

Top the chicken breast with guacamole and salsa. Garnish the rim of the plate with salsa verde and capsicum/sweet pepper, and sprinkle with coriander/cilantro. Serve on a bed of Mexican rice.

FAJITAS

SERVE 4

1 tablespoon oil
1 green capsicum/green sweet pepper,
  seeded and sliced
1 red capsicum/red sweet pepper,
  seeded and sliced
1 large onion, sliced
2 cups (500ml) fajita sauce (see page 116)

750g (1½ lb) chicken (or beef) strips
  (for beef add ¼ teaspoon
  baking powder/soda to tenderise)
12 x 15cm (6in) flour tortillas

MARINADE

1 tablespoon water
1 teaspoon mesquite seasoning
¼ cup olive oil

SIDE DISHES

shredded lettuce
guacamole (see page 12)
sour cream
pico de gallo (see page 84)
grated cheddar cheese
pickled jalapeños, chopped (optional)

- -

To make the marinade, combine the water, mesquite seasoning and olive oil in a bowl. Add the chicken strips and mix through thoroughly. Place in the refrigerator and marinate for a minimum of 1 hour.

Heat the oil in a wok on medium-high. Sauté the chicken for 5 minutes. Add the green and red capsicum/sweet peppers and onion and continue sautéing until the chicken is thoroughly cooked and the vegetables are still crisp. Stir through the fajita sauce.

Heat the tortillas in the microwave for approximately 30 seconds. Wrap the tortillas in a damp tea towel to keep them soft.

To serve, each person takes a tortilla, adds their favourite fillings and condiments, rolls up the tortilla and enjoys.

An alternative way to serve these is in a corn cup mould. Preheat oven to 180°C (350°F). In a pan, heat 1 cup of oil then lightly fry the tortilla on both sides for about 5 seconds (you are not crisping the tortilla yet, only allowing it to absorb some of the oil so that it can be worked with). In a deep ovenproof bowl, press the tortilla in so that it takes the shape of the bowl. Next, similar to blind baking, line tortilla with a piece of greaseproof paper and pour 2 cups of rice on top to hold tortilla in place. Bake in the oven for 10 minutes or until crisp.

Burrito Marimba

MAKES 6 BURRITOS

2 tablespoons mesquite seasoning
½ cup (125ml) olive oil
1kg (2lb) chicken breast fillets, roughly chopped
2 onions, chopped into chunks
2 capsicums/sweet peppers, (1 red and 1 green),
stalked, seeded and chopped into chunks
1 teaspoon oregano
1 teaspoon black pepper
50ml (2 fl oz) oil

½ cup tequila lime marinade (see page 108)
6 x 25cm (10in) flour tortillas
6 cups (1½ litres) chipotle chilli sauce
(see page 109)
2 cups (250g) grated cheddar cheese
sour cream for garnish
2 spring onions/scallions, finely chopped
for garnish

- -

Preheat oven to 180°C (350°F).

In a small bowl, mix the mesquite and olive oil. Place the chicken in a deep bowl and pour over the mesquite mix. Marinate for 1 hour.

Place the onion and capsicum/sweet pepper, on a baking tray and sprinkle with the oregano and black pepper. Pour the oil and tequila marinade over the top and mix through well. Place the tray in the oven and roast the vegetables for approximately 20 minutes, or until they are cooked. Be sure to mix the vegetables every 5 minutes so they do not burn.

Heat the oil in a wok on high. Stir-fry the chicken until cooked. Add the roasted vegetables and mix together. Place the tortillas on the bench and distribute the mixture evenly in the centre of each tortillas. Wrap into a parcel. Place the tortillas in a large casserole dish, cover with the chipotle sauce, sprinkle with the cheese and bake for 30 minutes. Garnish with sour cream and spring onions/scallions. Serve with frijoles and Mexican rice.

NOTE:
Burritos can be prepared in advance and refrigerated until required.

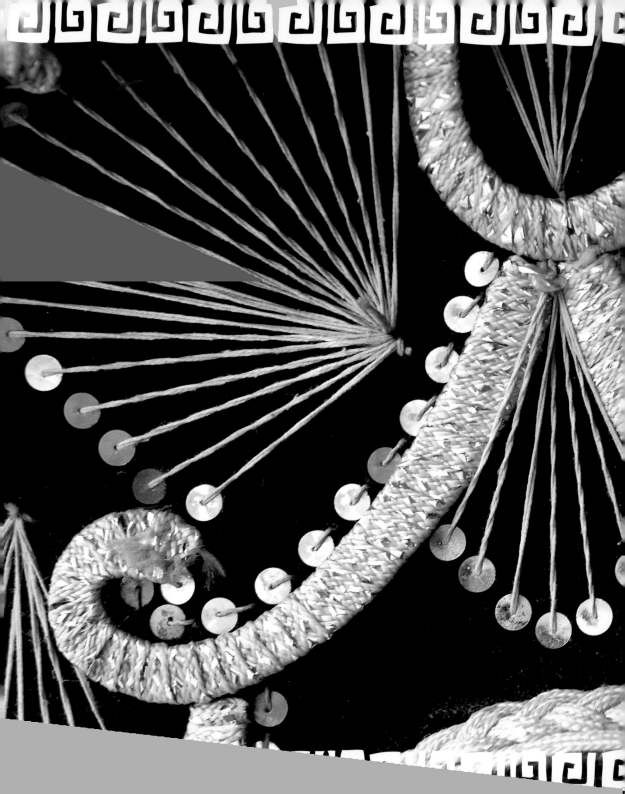

SEAFOOD

Ceviche of Spicy Scallops & Fish

SERVES 4

500g (1lb) fresh fish, boned and skinned
  (e.g. snapper, blue eye)
500g (1lb) fresh scallops and/or prawns/shrimp
juice of 6 limes (or enough to cover the fish)
1 small red chilli, finely chopped
1 small bunch of coriander/cilantro, chopped
zest of 2 limes

Salad
1 cucumber, diced
4 large red tomatoes, diced
1 small red onion, very finely sliced
1 tablespoon coriander/cilantro, chopped
2 spring onions/scallions, finely sliced
2 tablespoons white vinegar
dash of Tabasco sauce
salt and fresh ground pepper

To prepare the fish, wash the fish and scallops under the running tap and pat dry with paper towels or a tea towel. Slice the fish into chunks, about the same size as the scallops.

Place the lime juice, chilli and coriander/cilantro in a large bowl and mix. Add the seafood chunks and refrigerate for a minimum of 3–6 hours to allow the seafood to marinate through. The lime juice will 'cook' the seafood.

To make the salad, mix the salad ingredients together in a bowl.

To serve, evenly divide the salad on serving plates. Add the seafood mix and garnish with coriander/cilantro.

Burrito Del Mar

SERVES 4

1½ tablespoons margarine
1 onion, diced
⅓ (100g) plain/all purpose flour
200ml tomato salsa (see page 84)
3 cups (750ml) thickened cream
½ teaspoon salt
2 cups prawns/shrimp
200g (7oz) scallops
4 x 25cm (10in) flour tortillas
lemon wedges, to garnish

- -

In a large pot, melt margarine being careful not to burn it. Add the onion and flour then cook
for approximately 5 minutes. Add the tomato salsa, cream and salt and simmer until the mixture
thickens. Add the prawns/shrimp and scallops and cook for approximately 30 minutes on
low heat.

Warm the tortillas in the microwave for 30 seconds. Lay the tortillas on the bench and evenly
distribute the prawns/shrimp and scallops with a slotted spoon. Roll up tortilla and pour the
remaining sauce on top of the burrito.

Garnish with a wedge of lemon and serve with rice.

SPICY CALAMARI

SERVES 4

3 cups (750g) squid tail tubes
3 tablespoons olive oil
2 cloves garlic, crushed
2 red chillies diced
½ cup (125g) tomato salsa (see page 84)
1 tablespoon lemon juice
½ cup (125g) fresh coriander,/cilantro chopped for garnish
lemon wedges for garnish

Wash the squid (see Note below). Cut the squid into 5-cm (2-in) pieces and score with a sharp knife in a diamond design. Pat dry with paper towels. Put the pieces into a bowl and add the oil, garlic, chilli, tomato salsa and lemon juice. Cover with plastic wrap and marinate in the refrigerator for 2 hours. Drain the squid and reserve the marinade to use later as a sauce.

In a frying pan, sauté the squid over high heat for 3–4 minutes. Once cooked, serve immediately and drizzle calamari with the remaining marinade. Garnish with coriander/cilantro.

NOTE:

To clean squid, remove the head and tentacles so only the tail portion remains.

The tail tube portion contains a thin, clear sliver of cartilage that looks like a super-thin shard of glass. It is inedible and must be removed. Simply grasp the cartilage with your fingers and pull it from the squid body tube. It should release fairly easily.

The outer skin can be scraped or rubbed from the body tube under running water, leaving the white meat. On smaller, more tender squid, it is not necessary to remove the outer skin, but on larger squid the skin tends to toughen with cooking.

Rinse the meat inside and out under cold running water.

SIDES, SAUCES & MARINADES

MEXICAN RICE

MAKES 4 CUPS

¾ cup (180g) diced onions
¾ tablespoon crushed garlic
¼ cup (60ml) olive oil
2 cups white rice, washed and drained
1 x 400g (13oz) can crushed tomato
500ml (18 fl oz) vegetable stock
1 teaspoon cumin
½ teaspoon salt
1 tablespoon very finely chopped coriander/cilantro

- -

Heat the oil in a large pot on medium to high heat. Add the onion and garlic and sauté until the onion is translucent. Add the rice and stir well. Then add the tomato, stock, cumin and salt and mix thoroughly. Place the lid on the pot and cook on medium to low heat for approximately 20 minutes or until the liquid has been absorbed, stirring frequently. Add the coriander/cilantro and serve.

Note:
Coriander will wilt quickly so, for best results add just before serving. Mix thoroughly.

Tequila Lime Marinade

MAKES 150ML

100ml (3½ fl oz) lemon juice
25ml (1 fl oz) tequila
25ml (1 fl oz) water
¾ teaspoon garlic
½ teaspoon sugar
¼ teaspoon black pepper
½ teaspoon salt

- -

Put all the ingredients in a bottle or jar and shake well to combine.

Note:
Add ¼ cup (60ml) of olive oil to this marinade to make a zingy salad dressing.

Chipotle Chilli Sauce

MAKES 1 LITRE (33 FL OZ)

1 large onion, diced
1 teaspoon crushed garlic
30ml (1 fl oz) olive oil
1 x 400g (13oz) can crushed tomato
2 chipotle peppers in adobo sauce (available in tins from specialty suppliers)
2½ cups (625ml) water
1 tablespoon cornflour/cornstarch
1 teaspoon salt

- -

In a food processor add the onion and garlic and process until smooth. Heat the oil in a saucepan on high, add the onion and garlic puree and stir for 5 minutes.

Rinse the food processor, add the tomato and chilli and process until smooth. Add the tomato and chilli puree to the pot.

In a small bowl, mix the flour and ½ cup (125ml) water until smooth. Add to the pot.

Add the salt and rest of the water to the pot and bring the sauce to the boil. Simmer for 10 minutes. Remove the pot from the heat and cool. Blend the sauce with a bar mixer to get a smooth consistency.

It is a great tasting sauce that is suitable for serving with burritos or enchiladas. A small amount served with Burrito Del Mar gives this dish an extra zing.

Ranchera Sauce

MAKES APPROX 2 LITRES (67 FL OZ)

1 cup (250g) diced onions
150ml (¼ pint) oil
1 tablespoon garlic
⅓ cup plain/all purpose flour
6 cups (1.5 litres) water
2 x 400g (13oz) cans pureed tomato
¼ cup chilli powder
2 tablespoons salt
½ tablespoon cumin
1 tablespoon ground oregano
¼ tablespoon black pepper
¾ tablespoon sugar

- -

In a food processor, puree the onion until smooth.

Heat the oil in a large pot on medium heat. Add the onion and garlic and stir.

In a large bowl, add the flour and 2 cups (500ml) of the water and whisk until smooth, ensuring there are no lumps of flour. Add this to the pot and continue to cook for approximately 5 minutes. Then add the pureed tomato and stir through.

While this is cooking, in a large bowl add the chilli, salt, cumin, oregano, pepper and sugar with 2 cups of water and mix to combine. Add this mixture to the pot, stir through and cook over medium heat. Add the final 2 cups of water and bring to the boil. Simmer for 10 minutes. Remove the pot from the heat and let cool.

Blend the sauce with a bar mixer to ensure a smooth consistency. This sauce is great over beef enchiladas and burritos, grilled chicken, rice or even eggs.

Tomato Salsa (uncooked)

MAKES 1 LITRE (33 FL OZ)

1 large onion
1 large green capsicum
2 x 400g (13 oz) cans crushed tomato
¼ cup white vinegar
¼ teaspoon taco sauce seasoning
1 teaspoon salt
¼ cup water

In a food processor add the onion and capsicum and process. Use the pulse and do not leave on for too long. Place the puree in a mixing bowl.

Rinse the food processor and add the crushed tomato and process. Add the tomato puree to the mixing bowl and combine well. Add the taco sauce, seasoning, salt, vinegar and water and mix well.

This sauce is great as a dip, topping for nachos and frijoles, inside tacos or as a side dish for burritos and enchiladas.

Pico de Gallo (Chunky Salsa)

MAKES 3 CUPS

2 cups (220g) fresh diced tomatoes
½ cup (120g) finely diced onion
1 small fresh green Serrano chillies, chopped
1 sprig coriander/cilantro
30ml (1 fl oz) lemon juice
1 clove garlic, crushed
1 teaspoon salt
2 tablespoons white vinegar

In a large bowl, mix all the ingredients thoroughly. This is great with fajitas, tacos, frijoles.

Salsa Verde

MAKES 1 LITRE (33 FL OZ)

2 x 420g (14 oz) cans green tomatillos, drained (if tomatillos are unavailable,
  use 6 green tomatoes, stemmed)
1 teaspoon garlic
1 diced onion
2 fresh green Serrano chillies
2 tablespoons oil
½ cup (125ml) water
2 tablespoons coriander/cilantro, chopped
salt to taste (optional)

- -

If using green tomatoes: Place the tomatoes in a pot with enough water to just cover them.
Bring to the boil and cook until soft. Remove from the heat and drain in a colander.

In a food processor add the tomatillos or tomatoes, garlic, chilli and onion and process until
smooth.

Heat the oil in a pot on high heat. Add the tomatillo or tomato mix and the water and bring
to the boil. Simmer for approximately 10 minutes. Remove the pot from the heat and cool
completely. Add the coriander/cilantro. Blend the salsa again into a smooth sauce.

NOTE:
Tomatillos or husk tomatoes are small fruits (used as a vegetable) enclosed in a husk.
The fruit resembles a small unripe tomato and is usually green or yellow. The yellow
colour indicates ripeness but tomatillos are most often used when they are still green.

Fajita Sauce (uncooked)

MAKES 1 LITRE (33 FL OZ)

2 x 400g (13oz) cans crushed tomato
2 chipotle peppers in adobo sauce (available in tins from specialty suppliers)
1 teaspoon garlic
2 cups (500ml) water
¼ teaspoon salt

- -

Add all the ingredients to a food processor and blend. This sauce is used for fajitas.

Jalapeño Butter

MAKES 250G (8OZ)

½ teaspoon crushed garlic
1 tablespoon chopped jalapeños
¼ teaspoon cracked black pepper
¼ cup loosely packed fresh coriander/cilantro
250g (8oz) butter, softened

- -

Combine garlic and jalapeños in a food processor. Process until smooth; add coriander/cilantro, process until combined. Stir in butter. Using clingwrap, roll mixture into a log shape. Freeze. Cut off pieces as needed.

DRINKS

Red Wine Sangria

MAKES APPROX 2.5 LITRES (5 PINTS)

1 bottle (750ml or 1¼ pints) shiraz
1 cup triple sec
90ml (3 fl oz) lemon juice
90ml (3 fl oz) sugar syrup
90ml (3 fl oz) apple schnapps
4 cups (1 litre) soda water
2–3 cups of ice
½ an orange, chopped into wedges
½ an apple, chopped into wedges
½ a lemon, chopped into wedges

Sugar Syrup
Makes 2 cups
1 cup (250ml) sugar
1 cup (250ml) water

In a punch bowl or large jug add the shiraz, triple sec, lemon juice, sugar syrup, schnapps, soda water and ice and mix. Add the fruit wedges and serve.

To make the sugar syrup, place the sugar and water in a small pot and boil over a low heat until the sugar dissolves. Remove from the stove and cool.

Premium Hand-shaken Margarita

MAKES 1 GLASS

salt for frosting glass
1 cup ice
45ml (1½ fl oz) Gold tequila
30ml (1 fl oz) cointreau
60ml (2 fl oz) sweet and sour
15ml (½ fl oz) fresh lemon juice
lemon slice for garnish

Sweet & Sour
MAKES APPROX 1 LITRE (88 FL OZ)
3 cups (750ml) lemon juice
50ml lime juice
¾ cup (180ml) sugar
1 cup (250ml) water

Place enough salt onto a saucer to cover the base, about 2mm deep. Run a lemon wedge around the rim of each margarita glass and dip each glass in the salt to lightly coat just the rims. Set the glasses aside, upright.

To make the sweet and sour, place all the ingredients in a small pot and cook over a low heat until the sugar dissolves. Remove from the stove and cool. This mixture is used in many cocktails, including margaritas and sangria.

In a cocktail shaker, add the ice, tequila, cointreau, sweet and sour and lemon juice and shake until very cold. Using a cocktail strainer, strain the liquor into the prepared glass and garnish with a slice of lemon. Serve.

Frozen Lemon Margarita

MAKES 1 GLASS

salt for frosting glass
60ml (2 fl oz) gold tequila
30ml (1 fl oz) freshly squeezed lemon juice
30ml (1 fl oz) triple sec
1 cup ice
lemon slices for garnish

- -

Place enough salt onto a saucer to cover the base to about 2mm deep. Run a lemon wedge around the rim of each margarita glass and dip each glass in the salt to lightly coat just the rims. Set the glasses aside, upright.

In a blender add the tequila, lemon juice, triple sec and ice into a blender and blend until smooth. Pour into the prepared glass and garnish with lemon slices.

Frozen Strawberry Margarita

MAKES 4 GLASSES

sugar for frosting glasses
¾ cup (180ml) gold tequila
½ cup (125ml) freshly squeezed lemon juice
60ml (2 fl oz) triple sec
1 cup frozen strawberries
¼ cup caster sugar
8 cups ice
fresh strawberries for garnish

- -

Place enough sugar onto a saucer to cover the base to about 2mm deep. Run a lemon wedge around the rim of each margarita glass and dip each glass in the sugar to lightly coat just the rims. Set the glasses aside, upright.

Pour the tequila, lemon juice, triple sec, ice, strawberries and caster sugar to a blender and blend until smooth. Pour into the prepared glasses. Garnish with fresh strawberries.

MEXICAN PUNCH (NON-ALCOHOLIC)

MAKES 2 LITRES (3½ PINTS)

1½ cups (375ml) lemon cordial
½ cup (125ml) raspberry topping
6 cups (1½ litres) water
3 cups ice
lemon slices for garnish

- -

In a punch bowl or large jug, add all the ingredients and mix.

Chill and serve in tall glasses over the ice with the lemon slices.

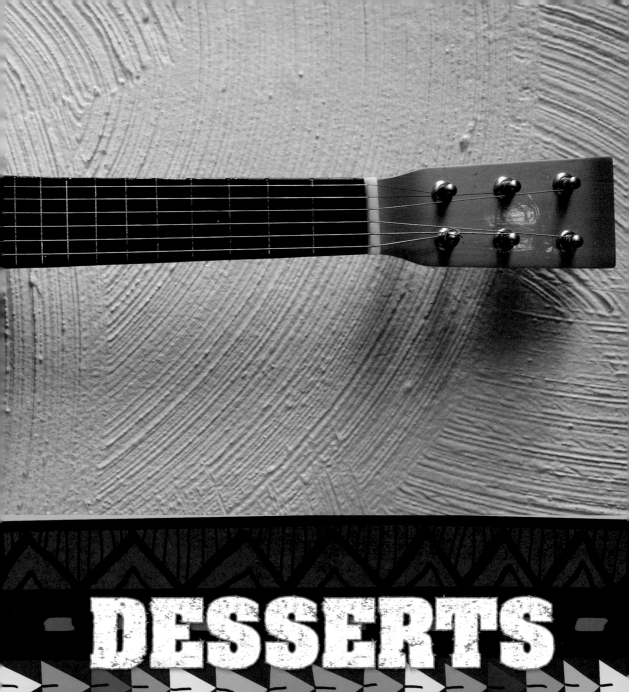

DESSERTS

MOUSSE DE TEQUILA

MAKES 8 GLASSES

4 eggs, separated
3 tablespoons fresh lime juice
2 tablespoons water
2 teaspoons unflavoured gelatine
1 cup sugar
pinch of salt
½ cup (125ml) thickened cream
¼ cup (60ml) silver tequila (the better the tequila the better the flavour)
¼ cup (60ml) triple sec
zest of 1 lime for garnish, finely grated, plus extra for garnish

- -

In a large bowl beat the egg yolks until thick and creamy. Add the lime juice, water, gelatine, sugar and salt and continue beating until well combined. Pour the mixture into a saucepan over medium heat and stir constantly for 5 minutes until the gelatine dissolves. Remove from the heat and stir in the cream, tequila, triple sec and lime zest. Transfer to a bowl and allow to cool. Refrigerate for 30 minutes.

In a large bowl, beat the egg whites until they form stiff peaks. Fold into the set gelatine mixture. Place in individual champagne or martini glasses. Place in the refrigerator to chill for at least 3 hours. Garnish with lime zest to serve.

CHURROS WITH HOT CHOCOLATE SAUCE

MAKES 20

125g butter, chopped
1 cup (150ml) water
1 cup plain/all purpose flour, sifted
3 eggs
vegetable oil to deep-fry
⅓ cup caster sugar
1½ teaspoons ground cinnamon
2 cups whipped cream

HOT CHOCOLATE SAUCE
5 cups (1.25 litres) thickened cream
350g (12oz) good-quality dark chocolate,
  chopped

In a small bowl, combine the caster sugar and cinnamon and shake onto a baking tray.

To make the churros, place butter and water in a saucepan over low heat. Cook, stirring occasionally, for 2 minutes or until the butter melts and water just comes to the boil. Add the flour and stir until well combined and the mixture comes away from the sides of the pan. Transfer to the bowl of an electric mixer and let cool slightly. Add the eggs, one at a time, beating well between each addition, until the mixture is smooth. Spoon the mixture into a piping bag fitted with a 1cm star nozzle.

Fill a deep frying pan with oil 4cm (1½in) deep and heat. (Oil is ready when a cube of bread browns in about 15 seconds.). Pipe 8cm x 10cm (3in x 4in) lengths of dough into the hot oil, using a knife to cut lengths. Cook for 1 minute each side. Remove and drain on paper towels. Immediately place the churros on the tray containing the sugar and cinnamon and toss gently to coat. Repeat with the remaining dough.

To make the hot chocolate sauce, combine the cream and chocolate in a saucepan over low heat. Cook, stirring occasionally, for 5 minutes or until the chocolate melts and mixture is hot. Serve the churros immediately with the hot chocolate sauce and fresh whipped cream on the side.

Apple Enchiladas

SERVES 4

4 Granny Smith (or other crisp, green) apples, sliced
2 tablespoons water
½ teaspoon cinnamon
2 tablespoons caster sugar
½ cup (125ml) apple schnapps
4 cinnamon tortillas (available at specialist grocers)
icing sugar/confectioners' sugar, to serve

- -

Preheat oven to 180°C (350°F).

In a saucepan, add the apple, water and sugar. Cover and simmer over a low heat for approximately 10–15 minutes until slightly stewed. Place the apple mix in a bowl and add the cinnamon and apple schnapps.

Lay the tortillas on a baking tray. Fill each tortilla evenly with the apple mix, place in the oven and bake for 10–15 minutes until golden.

Sprinkle the enchiladas with icing sugar/confectioners' sugar and serve with custard (see page150) and vanilla ice-cream.

Plantanitos Borrachos (Drunken Bananas)

SERVES 6

6 ripe bananas
¼ cup butter, cubed
1½ cups (375ml) sweet dessert wine
grated zest and juice of 1 orange
1 teaspoon cinnamon powder
1 tablespoon brown sugar
½ cup crushed almonds
whipped cream or vanilla ice cream to serve

- -

Preheat oven to 180°C (350°F).

Peel bananas and leave whole. Place in a casserole dish and pour in the dessert wine and orange juice and add butter. In a bowl, combine sugar, zest and cinnamon and sprinkle over the bananas. Cover the dish with foil and bake for 25 minutes until the bananas are soft but not mushy.

While this is cooking, lightly toast almonds in a dry frying pan over a medium heat until golden.

To serve, dish up the bananas, ladle any sauce left in the casserole dish, sprinkle with almonds and serve with whipped cream or ice-cream.

Index